Once upon a time, not so far away,

Sneaker the misguided dragon

stood guard over a very lonely

Princess Eyelet.

...bad-tempered, stubborn, and boastful!

Clearly, dragons did not make the best companions.

Eyelet made one last plea for Sneaker to
release her without a fight.

Humph

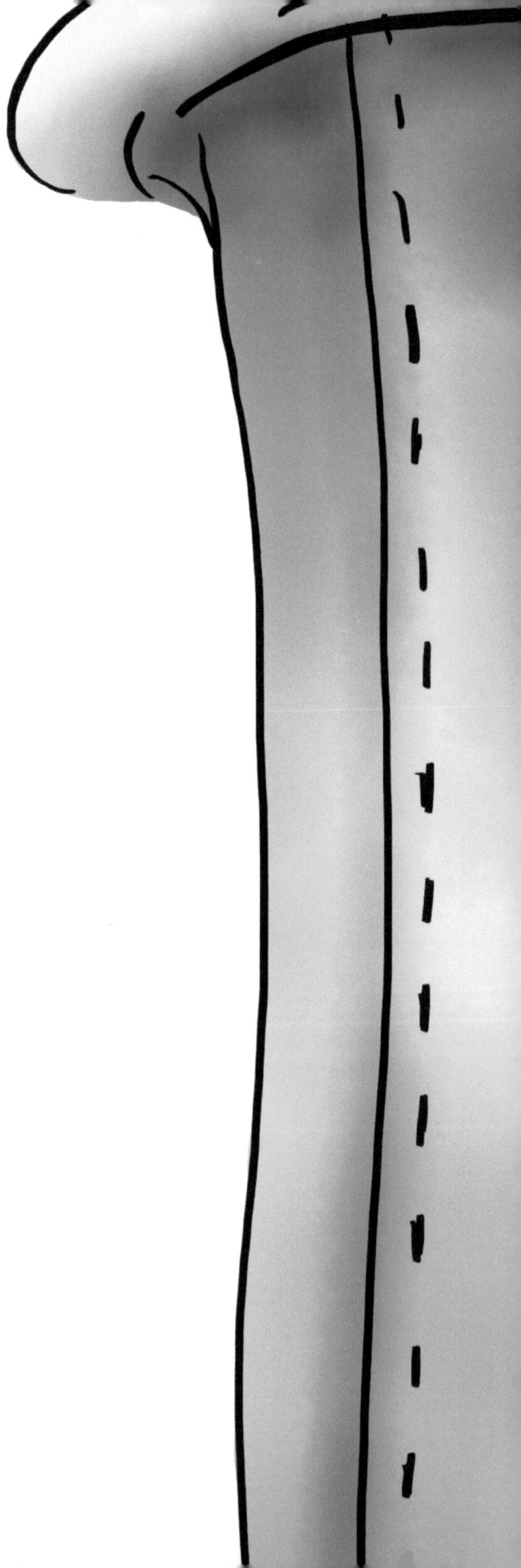

Well, asking nicely does not seem to work.

Gulp !

Sneaker roared,
sneered, and scoffed.

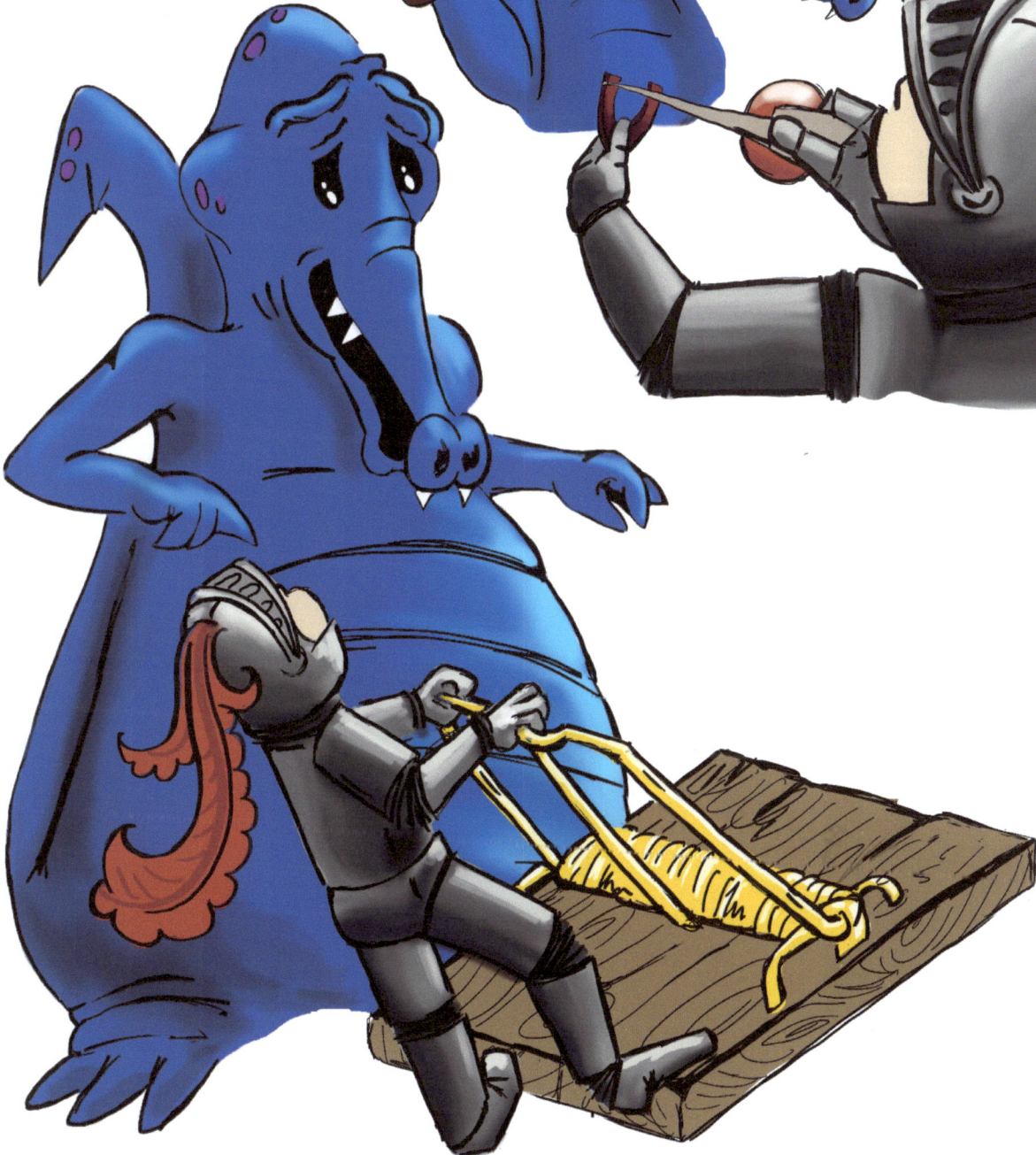

Now what ?

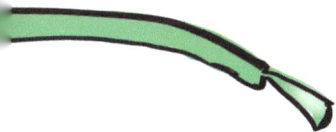

Quick!

Use the laces to tie Sneaker snug and tight!

Just like tying your shoes.

Instep gawked at his feet.

Um, well... the thing is ....
knights don't have shoe laces.

Eyelet thought a moment and called
down from the tower.

Around the dragon.

Through his legs.

Now pull the laces tight!

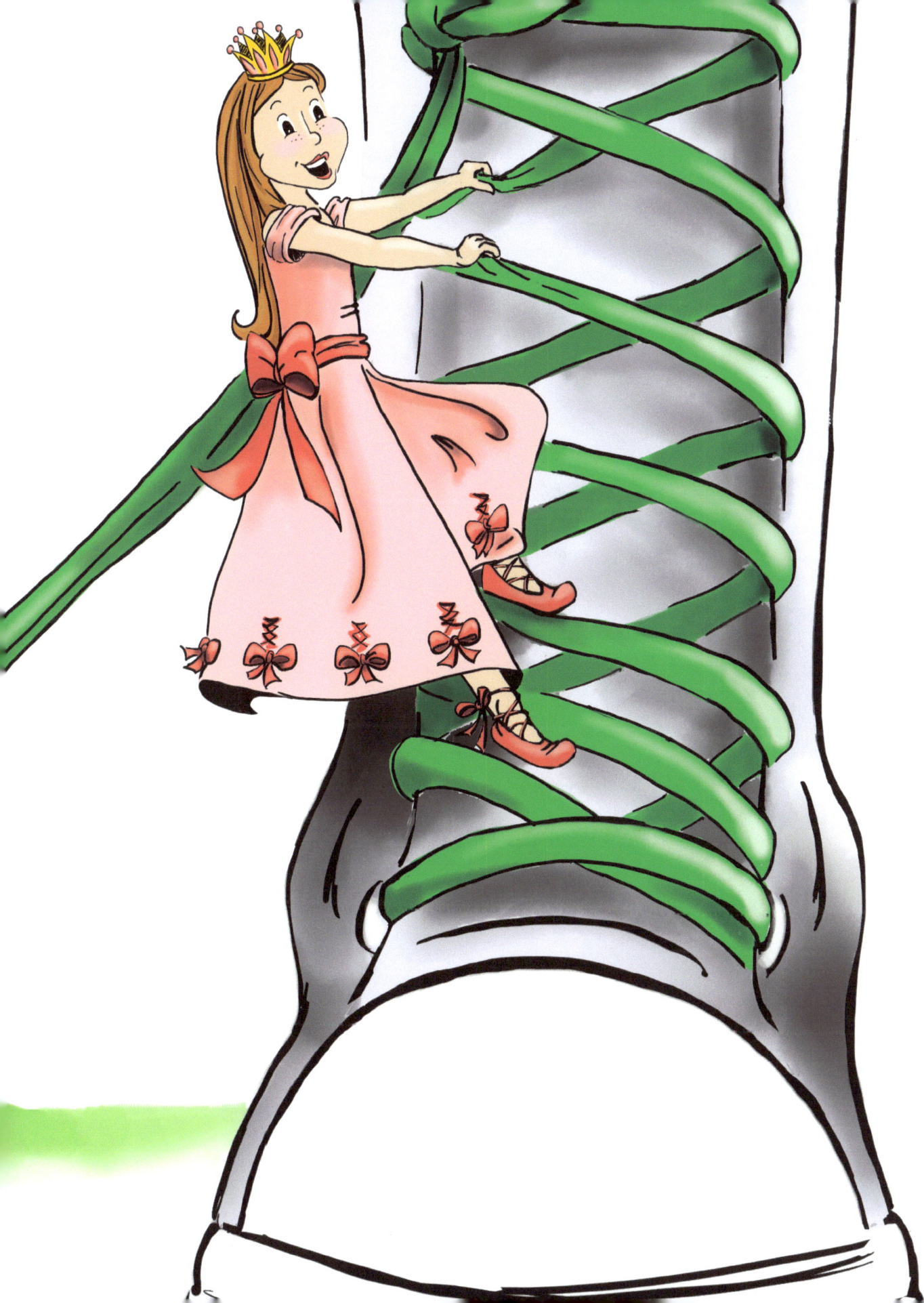

I can be good.
I promise.

Well, every adventure could use a towering, fire-breathing dragon.

And so began a friendship of the
most unlikely kind.

Make your
dragon

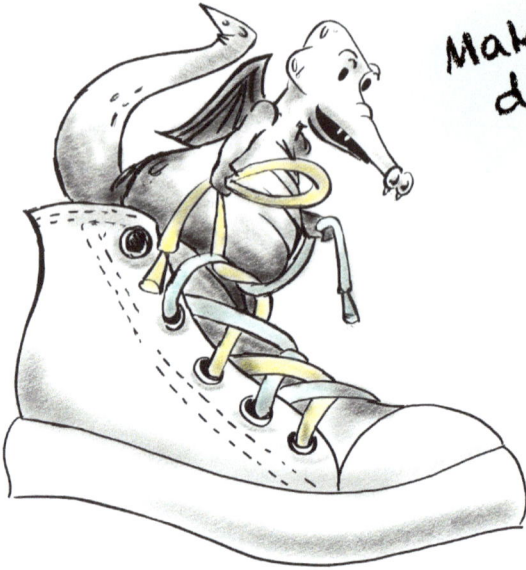

Around the
dragon

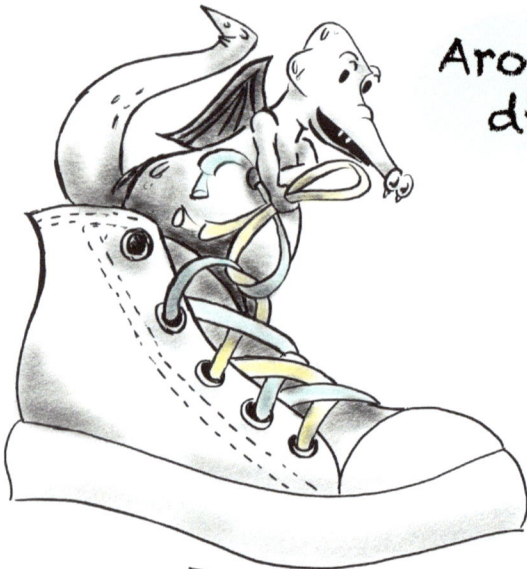

Through
his legs

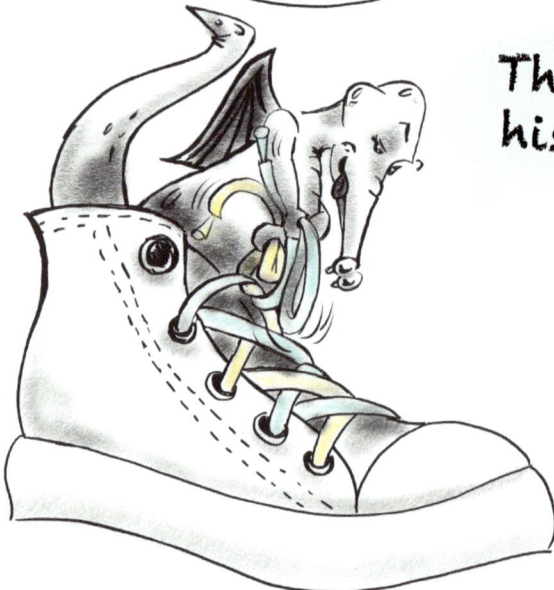

Pull the laces
TIGHT

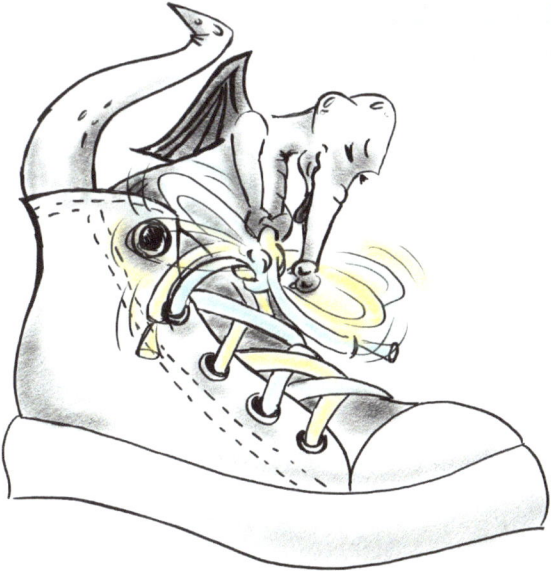

Snug and Tight!
(To the tune of "Over the River and Through the Woods")

Around the dragon,
and through his legs.

Now pull the laces tight!

This is the way
the laces will stay
all through the day and night.

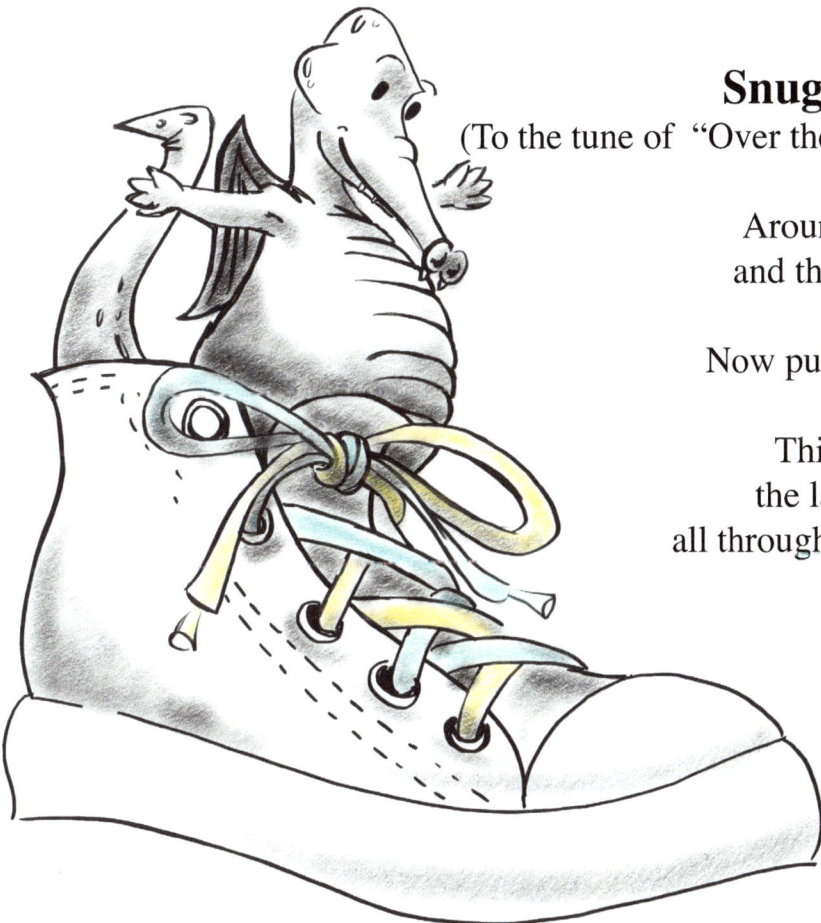

videos and downloads
visit us at
pickleandbug.com

www.ingramcontent.com/pod-product-compliance
Lightning Source LLC
LaVergne TN
LVHW072100070426

835508LV00002B/189